Contents

PUPPETS AND SHADOW PLAYS

Change a sock into a lively hand puppet. With a little sewing, a little decorating, and a lot of imagination, you can make a dragon, a princess, a soldier, or any puppet character you want. Transform a glove and a styrofoam ball into another type of puppet. Create a variety of puppet people. Build your own puppet stage. Put on your own puppet show . . . or act out the play, A FINE MESS. Either way, you and your friends will have fun.

All these activities, and many more, are included in this book. Acting is fun. Before long you will be writing and producing your own shows. You can amaze your friends with the animal shadows you can make with your hands. Amuse people with the fun-filled people shadow play, DR. DIN'S DISASTER.

It's fun to make original puppets and stick shadow figures. Make some for yourself. Make some to give to your friends. Most of the puppets can be made with materials you will find around the house.

The pictures in this book help you see each step of a project. Most of the work you can do by yourself or with your friends, but sometimes you may have to ask for help. If you can't do it alone, ask your older brother or sister, your parents, or your teacher to help.

Here are a few hints to get your puppet and shadow plays off the ground.

- Select a time and place for your show.
- Make sure you have everything you need for your show . . . puppets, scenery, props.
- Know your lines and plan your performance carefully.
- Practice . . . practice . . . practice. The more you practice the better your play will be.

Let your creative self go! You are the actor. Practice changing your voice. Each of your characters should have a character and voice of its own. Plan carefully and you and your audience are sure to have a good time.

HAVE FUN WITH THE FUN TIME BOOKS

Basic Sock Puppet

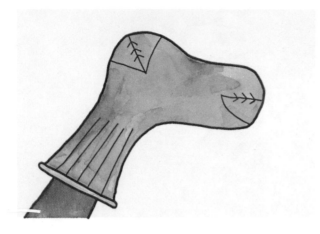

PUT a brightly colored sock on your hand. The heel should be on top of your wrist.

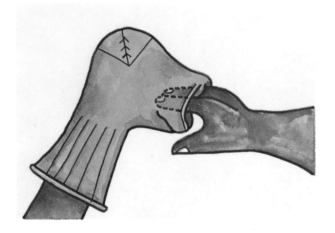

STUFF the toe back toward your palm. This makes the puppet's mouth.

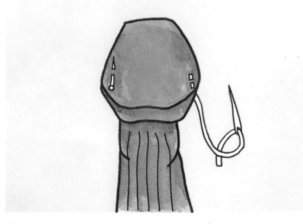

PIN the corners of the mouth. Take the sock off and sew the corners. This holds the mouth in place.

8

SEW buttons on for eyes and nose.

ADD ears, if you like. They can be any funny shape. Cut them from cloth and sew them on.

Some other things you can use are sequins for eyes. Try string, yarn, or felt for hair.

You can make almost any kind of animal you want. Try different ones.

9

Boy Sock Puppet

TAKE a basic sock puppet.

SEW some rickrack in his mouth for teeth.

SEW on loops of bright, heavy yarn. Put them all around his face for a mane.

PRACTICE moving your fingers inside to make him look sad, happy, or mean.

Girl Sock Puppet

TAKE a basic sock puppet.

MAKE little eyelashes of black yarn. Sew them over her button eyes. Trim them carefully.

SEW long pieces of yarn on top of her head. Heavy gift wrapping yarn works well. Part it in the middle and braid it if you like. Tie on bright bows.

PRACTICE having her sing a song.

Basic Glove Puppet

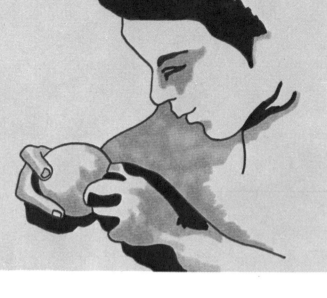

TAKE a styrofoam ball for the puppet head.

MAKE a hole a little larger than your finger. Use a kitchen knife for this.

WRAP a small piece of cardboard around your finger and glue it. Then glue this piece of cardboard in the hole like a neck.

GLUE black dot eyes on.

DRAW a mouth with a felt tip pen.

GLUE on hair of yarn, felt, or fake fur.

DRAW a pattern on paper to fit your own hand. Spread your thumb and first two fingers apart. Make it too big so you'll have room to sew around the edges.

PIN this pattern on cloth. Then cut out two. Pin them together.

SEW these together along the dotted lines. Then turn this inside-out.

GLUE this "body" to the cardboard neck.

You can add collars, scarves, buttons, capes, and all kinds of decorations.

Boy Glove Puppet

TAKE a basic glove puppet.

GLUE a bit of fake fur on his head for hair.

DRAW a big happy smile on his face.

CUT a pointy collar from felt and glue it on.

SEW bright buttons down his front.

Lady Glove Puppet

TAKE a basic glove puppet.

MAKE her hair out of curly strips of paper. Glue it on her head.

CUT a long cape from bright cloth. Put it around her shoulders. Fasten it in front with an old piece of jewelry. (Ask your mother before you borrow it.)

CUT two pieces of old lace. Glue them around the two "hands" for cuffs.

Props

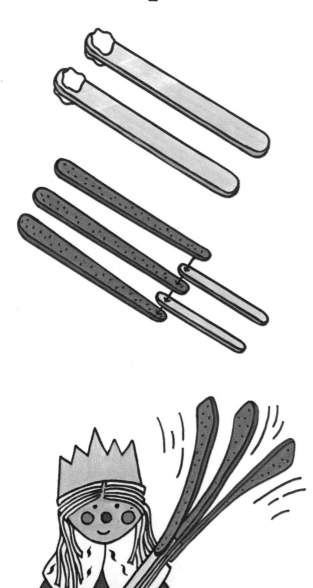

Slapstick

GET three of the longest emery boards you can find and two popsicle sticks.

COVER both sides of each popsicle stick with glue — for about an inch.

MAKE an emery board/popsicle stick sandwich. Glue them all together. Use the narrow end of the emery boards.

MAKE SURE all the emery boards are even at the top.

LET DRY.

Now a puppet can hold the popsicle end and hit another puppet over the head. It makes a much louder noise!

Crown

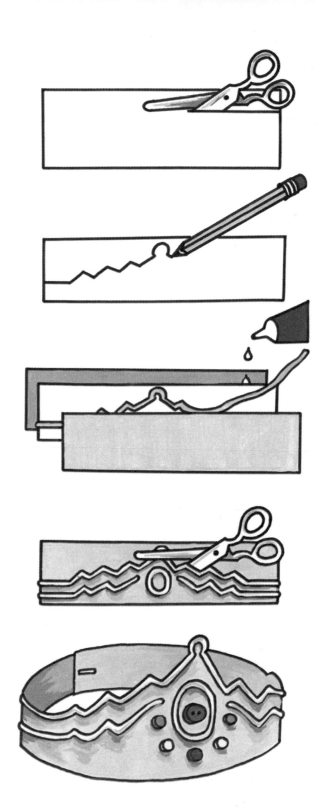

CUT a strip of heavy paper and two strips of aluminum foil the same size.

DRAW an outline of a crown on the heavy paper. Make it higher in the center and smaller on the ends.

GLUE string along the drawn outline of the crown. Then glue more string in pretty patterns.

GLUE foil to each side of the heavy paper.

PRESS foil gently around the string pattern.

CUT above string outline.

OVERLAP the ends so it fits your puppet's head. Then staple the ends together.

You can add buttons, sequins, or beads. Put them on with glue.

Puppet Stage

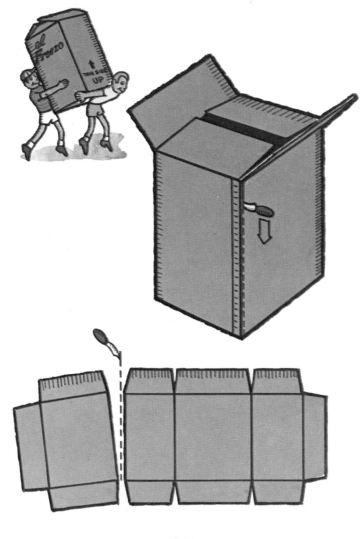

GET a large cardboard carton from an appliance store. The best kind is one from a refrigerator or freezer.

CUT down the corner where the box is stapled together. Then lay the box flat on the floor.

CUT OFF the widest side. Save this.

STAND the three sides up. Bend the box back so the inside is out.

MARK and CUT four or five small X's on each flap of the side you cut off.

HOLD this side across the back near the top of the other three.

BEND the flaps over the sides.

MARK and CUT small X's to match in the sides of the stage.

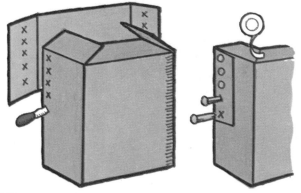

PUSH paper fasteners through the holes and spread them apart to hold the back of the stage to the sides.

BEND the top and bottom flaps back. Tape them together with some strong tape.

MARK the place for the stage opening near the top of the front of the stage. The opening must be wide enough to have four puppets show.

CUT out the stage opening carefully.

GET a 1 inch by 2 inch board that is about 6 inches longer than the front of the stage. This is the board for the curtain.

LAY the board across the front of the stage about 2 inches above the opening.

MARK lines of the stage sides at the top and bottom of the board.

CUT a slot 1 inch wide between the marks.

SLIP first one end of the board through a slot from inside the stage. Then slip the other end through the slot on the other side. The ends should stick out evenly on each side.

PAINT the stage with poster paint.

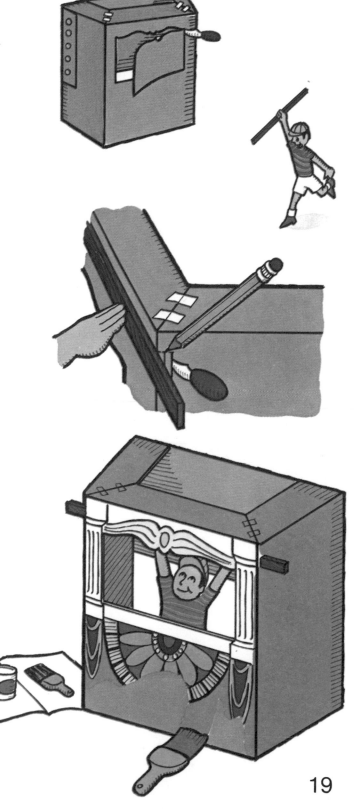

19

Stage Backdrop

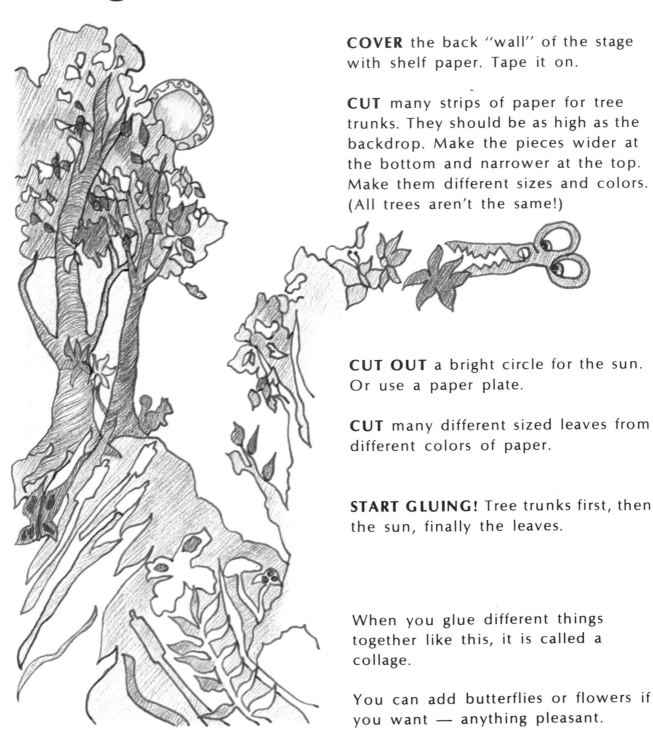

COVER the back "wall" of the stage with shelf paper. Tape it on.

CUT many strips of paper for tree trunks. They should be as high as the backdrop. Make the pieces wider at the bottom and narrower at the top. Make them different sizes and colors. (All trees aren't the same!)

CUT OUT a bright circle for the sun. Or use a paper plate.

CUT many different sized leaves from different colors of paper.

START GLUING! Tree trunks first, then the sun, finally the leaves.

When you glue different things together like this, it is called a collage.

You can add butterflies or flowers if you want — anything pleasant.

CUT OUT some bright-colored mushrooms.

TAPE them to the front of your stage. Masking tape works well.

Working Curtain

FIND a piece of cloth about 4 inches wider and 6 inches longer than the stage opening.

MEASURE and MARK every 4 inches down one edge (on the back). Do the same thing on the other edge. Then connect the marks opposite each other.

LAY a ruler across this line. Mark 1 inch from each edge. Mark in the middle also. Repeat this on each line.

CUT slits above and below each dot. Make these slits very tiny.

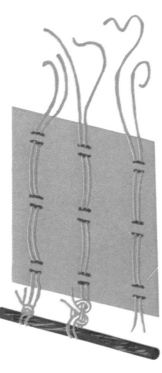

MEASURE three strings — 2-1/2 times as long as the curtain.

DOUBLE one string and thread it through the first row of slits. Repeat with the next string in the next row of slits. Keep doing this.

TIE the bottom ends of the strings around a heavy dowel rod.

WRAP the bottom of the curtain around the dowel. Glue it well. This is the curtain weight.

STAPLE the top edge to the curtain support.

SCREW in a screw eye above each of the three strings.

THREAD each string through the screw eye above it. Then go across through the ones to the right.

SCREW in a fourth screw eye on the far right. All the strings come to this. Pull all at once to raise the curtain.

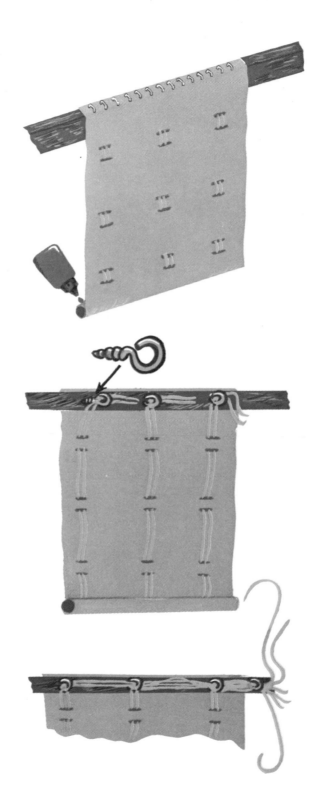

A Play

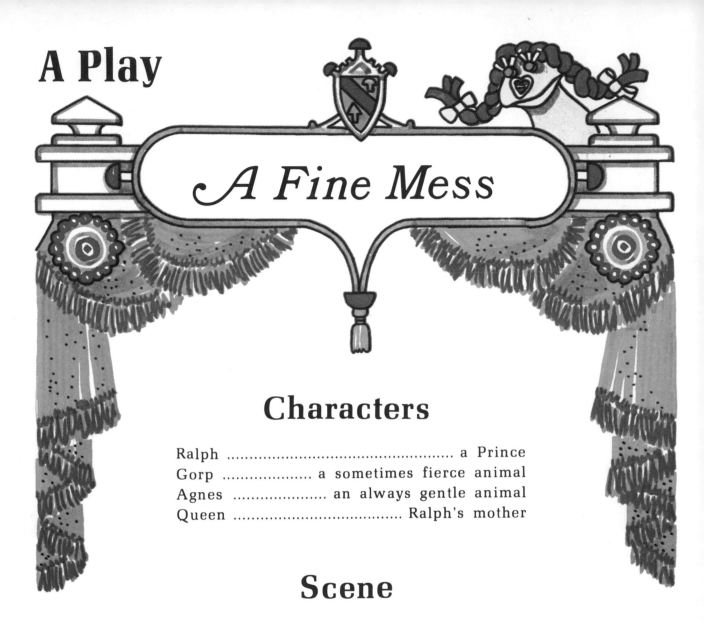

A Fine Mess

Characters

Ralph .... a Prince
Gorp .... a sometimes fierce animal
Agnes .... an always gentle animal
Queen .... Ralph's mother

Scene

In the kingdom — mostly forest — on a pleasant day.

Gorp is onstage as the curtain opens. Ralph enters humming softly.

GORP: *(Doesn't hear Ralph.)* Growl! Roar! Today I'm going to practice being fierce. Roar! Growl! I'm tired of being a nice guy. Roar!

RALPH: Hi. What are you doing? You sound pretty silly.

GORP: Don't say that! I'm mean and fierce.

RALPH: You look kind of nice to me. Do you want to play?

GORP: Play? The nerve of you asking me if I want to play. I'm going to eat you. *(He grabs Ralph by the head. Gorp drags Ralph offstage making gobbling noises as he goes.)*

AGNES: *(Enters looking all around.)* Gorp. Gorp. Where are you?

GORP: *(Returning.)* Here I am. What do you want?

AGNES: I've been looking all over the kingdom — mostly forest — for you. There's an emergency. What have you been doing? Where have you been?

GORP: I've been right here — practicing being fierce. Roar! Growl!

AGNES: Stop it Gorp. I've told you that is ridiculous. You don't have to be fierce to impress people. Anyway, there is a real problem and we need your help. So please be serious.

GORP: What is it? What is wrong?

AGNES: The Prince is missing.

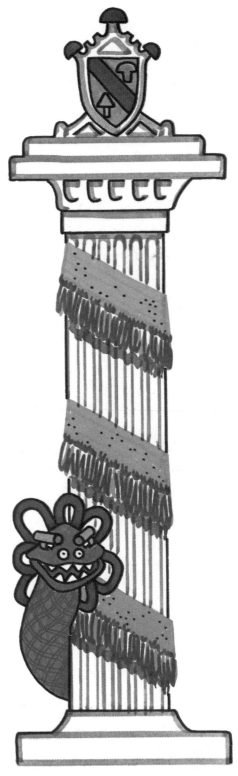

GORP: The Prince, hmmmm . . .

AGNES: He's missing.

GORP: Missing, hmmmm . . .

AGNES: His name is Ralph.

GORP: Ralph, hmmmm . . . *(Directly to audience.)* Who ever heard of a prince named Ralph?

AGNES: Shape up, Gorp! This is serious. We have to find the Prince.

GORP: I'll find him. I'll save him. I'll be fierce! Roar! What does he look like?

AGNES: He's quite small. And he wears a crown.

GORP: Is a crown like a kind of hat?

AGNES: Yes, sort of.

GORP: Is it sharp?

AGNES: I guess you could say that.

GORP: I think I ate him.

AGNES: You ate him?

GORP: I ate him. I was being fierce.

AGNES: That's terrible. This is a fine mess you've got us into!

GORP: I just wanted to impress everyone.

AGNES: Well, it's bound to impress the Queen. Here she comes.

QUEEN: *(Entering.)* I have been looking all over the entire kingdom — mostly forest — for my son, Ralph, the Prince.

GORP: I ate him.

AGNES: He ate him.

QUEEN: You ate him?!! *(Queen beats Gorp over the head with a slapstick.)*

AGNES: Your Highness. Control yourself. You are not behaving like a queen!

QUEEN: Forgive me. I was overcome with grief. You have eaten my only son, Ralph.

GORP: Well — not really. I was just pretending. I wanted to impress everyone. I was being fierce. Roar! Were you impressed? *(The Queen moves toward Gorp. She raises the slapstick.)*

QUEEN: YES! *(Queen beats Gorp on the head with the slapstick.)* What have you done with my son, Ralph, the Prince? *(She stops beating.)*

GORP: I just chewed on him a little bit around the edges. But I made a lot of noise. *(Queen raises the slapstick.)* He's okay. He's over there — under the fifth toadstool to the right.

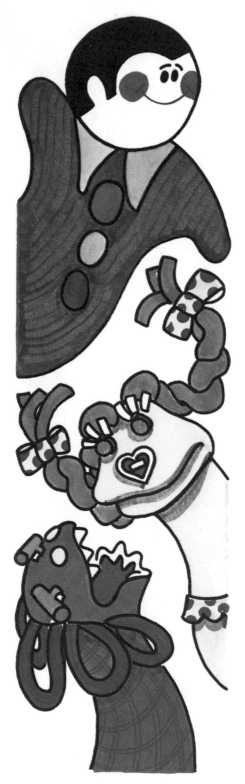

QUEEN: My son, Ralph, the Prince — come here. *(Ralph enters, without his crown.)*

QUEEN: Ralph, where is your crown? Everyone knows that you cannot be a prince without a crown.

GORP: *(To Agnes.)* A crown is a kind of sharp hat? Right?

AGNES: Right.

GORP: I ate it.

AGNES: *(To Queen.)* He ate it.

QUEEN: You ate it?!! *(Queen beats Gorp over the head with the slapstick.)*

RALPH: Mother! Control yourself. You are not behaving like a queen!

QUEEN: Forgive me. I am upset. You have eaten my only son's only crown.

RALPH: *(Looking into Gorp's open mouth.)* No he hasn't. Look in here.

AGNES: Let me see. *(Agnes looks down Gorp's throat.)* Amazing. Imagine that! It was so sharp, it got stuck.

RALPH: I'm too small to reach it.

QUEEN: What is this foolish business?

AGNES: The crown is on his tooth.

RALPH: My crown is on his tooth.

QUEEN: Your crown is on his tooth?!! *(Queen starts toward Gorp to beat him with the slapstick.)*

GORP: Don't let her near me. She doesn't behave like a queen.

RALPH: Forgive her. The excitement is too much for her.

QUEEN: Call the royal dentist!

AGNES: No need, Your Highness. *(Directly to the audience.)* I moon-light as the tooth fairy. Gorp, open wide.

(Agnes almost disappears down Gorp's big mouth. Gorp makes terrible groaning and choking noises. They push and pull, back and forth, across the stage. Finally, Agnes holds the crown high.)

AGNES: HERE IT IS!

RALPH: YEA!

QUEEN: This is simply too much. *(She leaves.)*

RALPH: This was fun. I'll be back again tomorrow to play. But I'll leave my crown at home. Goodby. *(He leaves.)*

AGNES: This was a fine mess you got me into.

GORP: At least it was a royal mess. And I was very fierce. And the Queen was certainly impressed. Tomorrow, I'll be even fiercer! Roar!

(The curtain closes.)

This play is like a pattern for you. Now you can write your own play.

SHADOW PLAYS

Hand Shadows

STAND so your hands are between a light and a bare wall. Use your fingers and arms to make animals on the wall.

Rabbit

MAKE a V with your first two fingers. These are the rabbit's ears.

BEND DOWN your other two fingers. Put your thumb on top of them with your knuckle sticking out a little.

WIGGLE the ears back and forth.

Butterfly

CROSS your hands with your thumbs in the middle. Your palms should be toward you.

WAVE your fingers back and forth to make the wings move.

32

Eagle

BEND your left elbow up straight and your wrist down. Curve the ends of your fingers just a little.

LEAVE a space between your thumb and your fingers. Keep your thumb straight.

PUT your right arm next to the left. Bend your elbow the same way. Bend your right wrist so your hand is on top of your left hand.

HOOK your middle fingers in the space between your left fingers and thumb. Keep your first finger and little finger out straight.

Grouchy Dog

HOLD OUT one hand with your first finger bent back. Bend your thumb so it touches the top of this finger.

KEEP your other fingers straight. Move your little finger down so there is a space between your fingers.

TRY some animals of your own. Maybe you can make a dragon, an elephant, or some really strange beast.

Cat

USE both hands and one arm. Make a fist with your two middle fingers and your thumb tucked in.

BEND your first finger and little finger but let them stick up.

USE your other hand to hold your arm just above the elbow. Point your first finger to make a tail.

Bull

PUT the backs of your hands together. Do this so the left one is near the top of the right one.

CUP the fingers of your right hand.

CURVE your left thumb and first finger toward each other. Bend your fingers all the way down to your palm.

34

People Shadows

FIND a very large doorway or archway. Hang an old white sheet across it for a screen. If you're using a stage, close the curtains part way. Hang the sheet between the curtains.

TIE strings to the top corners to hold the sheet. Hook these to the top of the doorway.

TAPE the bottom corners of the sheet to the floor. Stretch the sheet enough to keep it from wrinkling.

MAKE scenery from cardboard or paper. Tape or pin the scenery right to the screen.

KEEP the scenery on the outside edges of the screen to give the actors room to move.

USE a record player or tape recorder to play background music. You can tape other sounds too. Or have someone offstage make sound effects.

MAKE costumes from anything you can find. Only the outline will show. They don't have to look nice backstage.

TRY an old newspaper for a skirt or a hat. A sword can be cut from a piece of cardboard.

PUT a large light without a shade behind the screen. Place it so the light shines on the screen.

STAND so the audience always sees a side view of you. Keep a little space between you and other things that are behind the screen.

MAKE your movements big and simple. Small movements won't show.

LOOK at the top of your light bulbs. The larger the numeral, the brighter the light will be.

USE a large numeral when you want a sharp shadow. A smaller numeral will make a soft shadow.

TRY more than one light. Put them at different angles behind the screen. You might want to use some small and some large bulbs.

EXPERIMENT with lights. You can change dwarfs to giants. You can even make people disappear.

TURN OUT the other lights in the room when you are ready to begin. Turn off the lights behind the screen at the end. Turn on the room lights.

37

Whose Shadow?

PLAY a game behind your shadow screen.

CHOOSE some people everyone in the audience knows about. Let the audience guess whose shadow you are.

KEEP the lights behind the screen turned off until each person is set. Then turn them on and begin the action. Have the rest of the room dark.

PRETEND to be a clown. Put an old mop on your head. Wear a funnel on the mop.

CUT a hole in a rubber ball and stick it on your nose. Make some ruffles from newspapers. Tie them on your ankles and wrists.

TURN yourself into a witch. Make a pointed hat from a paper circle. Glue it together to make a cone.

GIVE yourself a long pointed paper nose. Tape it on. Pin an old blanket around your shoulders.

38

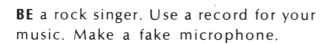

BE a rock singer. Use a record for your music. Make a fake microphone.

HAVE a whole rock group if you like. Pin cutouts of an organ or drums on the screen. Use a cardboard guitar.

THINK of other people you can pretend to be. Turn out the lights behind the screen when the audience guesses who you are.

CHANGE the game by having the audience guess what you are doing. Have a pretend football game or a wedding.

GO FISHING and catch a fish that is too large to pull in. Fall backward when you finally land it.

THINK of other things to pretend behind your shadow screen. How many times can your audience guess right?

Stick Shadows

CUT some side view puppets from cardboard. Give them funny noses and chins if you want.

GLUE the puppets on sticks or long, thin pieces of heavy cardboard.

MAKE your puppets in color by cutting out the center. Leave a small frame around the edge.

GLUE colored tissue paper or cellophane over the back of the cut out spot. When the light shines through the paper, the color will show on the screen.

FIND something to use for a stage. Almost anything will work as long as you can hide behind the bottom of it.

TRY a cardboard box stage, a window, a doorway, or a table.

STRETCH a piece of white material or tissue paper across the part you want to use for a screen. Cover the bottom with dark paper or material.

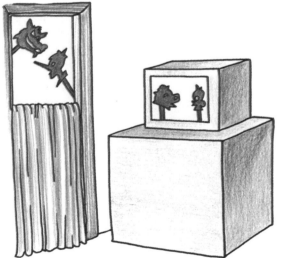

PUT a light behind your stage. Make it shine on the screen. A flashlight will work for a small stage.

USE a light without a shade for a larger stage.

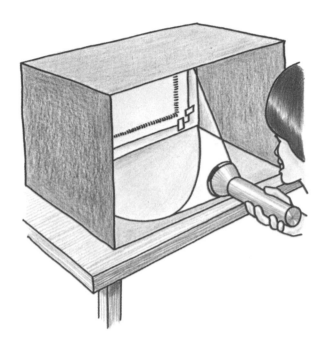

HOLD the puppets between the light and the screen to make a shadow. When they are close to the screen the shadow will be the size of the puppet.

MOVE the puppets back to stretch out the shadows. Try moving them around to see the magic effects you can get.

BE CAREFUL not to let anything get between the light and the puppet. It will block out the shadow.

MAKE the puppets talk in different voices. Or get a friend to help you.

FIND a play you can use in a book. Better yet, make up your own play.

41

Dr. Din's Disaster

HAVE a shadow play comedy. Use a large screen. Set up a table behind the screen.

TURN a bathrobe into a doctor's coat. Put on a knit hat.

STUFF the toes of an old pair of nylons with newspapers. Pull them over your shoes so the stuffing is at the end of your toes.

TAPE them around your ankles. The shadows will look like big floppy shoes.

CUT a large saw from cardboard. Use it to pretend to cut the patient's stomach open.

FIND a record with scary music. Put it on the record player. Have it ready to start when the play begins.

TIE a lot of scarves or rags together. Make a string about 10 feet long. Get a pair of gloves that are much too big for you.

GATHER some funny objects like a large rubber spider on a piece of elastic. Try a toy dog or cat. Get a big plastic flower.

HIDE all the objects on the edge of the table before the play begins. Coil the scarf string so an end can easily be pulled out.

WRITE some funny lines about the operation. Maybe you would like to start out by saying that Dr. Din is doing a stomach operation on rich Mr. Pennyworth Bolt.

TELL about each body part that is being taken out. Put in some lines about what strange things the patient ate for lunch.

GO ON from there. Write down anything that seems funny to you.

ASK someone to read the lines while the operation is going on. He should stand on the other side of the screen so he can be heard.

FIND a friend who will be your patient. Ask him to lie on the table so he hides the funny objects.

TURN on the lights when you are ready to begin. Remember to stand so the audience gets a side view of you.

TURN ON the music. Keep it soft so the reader and the other sounds can be heard.

PICK UP the gloves. Hold out your arms. Slowly put on the gloves.

HOLD your saw in the air. Then pretend to cut open the patient's stomach.

PULL the hidden objects out one at a time. Lift them up slowly. Hold them in the air for a second. Then quickly throw each one over your shoulder.

HAVE a metal wastebasket full of empty tin cans hidden offstage. Get someone to drop it each time you throw an object.

REMOVE all the patient's insides. When you are finished, sew him back up.

USE a giant needle made from cardboard. Put a piece of twine through the eye. Pretend to sew your coat in.

END the play by running out in front of the screen. Yell, "Oh no, I've operated on the wrong man." Use your imagination and have fun.

THIS IS WHAT OTHERS SEE!

INDEX

ILLUSTRATORS

About the Editors

Cameron John and Margaret A. Yerian have advanced degrees in psychology and mass communications from the University of Michigan. They have been active in educational and instructional writing for both adults and children, with many publications to their credit. Their work has ranged from the Educational Television Project in American Samoa, where Mrs. Yerian served as a producer/director and Mr. Yerian was a writer and editor to their present work as media consultants in the Detroit metropolitan area.